ID0467558

TENDER THE MAKER

May Swenson
Poetry Award Series
Volume 18

TENDER THE MAKER

poems
by

Christina Hutchins

UTAH STATE UNIVERSITY PRESS
Logan

© 2015 Christina Hutchins
Foreword © 2015 Cynthia Hogue

Published by Utah State University Press
An imprint of University Press of Colorado
5589 Arapahoe Avenue, Suite 206C
Boulder, Colorado 80303

   The University Press of Colorado is a proud member of
the Association of American University Presses.

The University Press of Colorado is a cooperative publishing enterprise supported, in part,
by Adams State University, Colorado State University, Fort Lewis College, Metropolitan
State University of Denver, Regis University, University of Colorado, University of
Northern Colorado, Utah State University, and Western State Colorado University.
Manufactured in the United States of America

∞ This paper meets the requirements of the ANSI/NISO Z39.48-1992 (Permanence
of Paper).

Publication credits appear on page 66,
which constitutes an extension of this copyright page.

Cover series design by Barbara Yale-Read
Cover photo "Drawbridge to the City (Rothenburg 1965)" by Bruce Hutchins. Used by
permission.

ISBN 978-1-60732-438-6 (paper)
ISBN 978-1-60732-439-3 (ebook)
DOI: 10.7330/9781607324393

Library of Congress Cataloging-in-Publication Data
Hutchins, Christina, 1961-
  [Poems. Selections]
  Tender the maker : poems / by Christina Hutchins.
    pages ; cm. — (May Swenson, poetry award series ; Volume 18)
   ISBN 978-1-60732-438-6 (cloth) — ISBN 978-1-60732-439-3 (ebook)
  I. Title.
  PS3558.U826A6 2015
  811'.54—dc23
                                       2015012978

for the makers who grieve

CONTENTS

Again and again in Christina Hutchins's exquisite *Tender the Maker*, poems startle us into awareness of the overlooked, the nearly-always invisible (such as a library's unused dictionary), and the marvelous, those aspects of life that come under the rubric of "mystery," in all senses of the word. Hutchins combines a pitch-perfect and precise lyricism with a postmodern sensibility of language's materiality. Take "Between Pages of the Dictionary" as an example, the first quatrain of which I'll quote in full:

> Lift away *lurk* and let *lowbrow* breathe . . .
> Language has lingered into slow scents: a library's
> mottle-storming dust, cupcake breath,
> inked leather. A luna moth left too long.

The opening of an old dictionary leads to a rich dwelling on the thing itself, the actual book and the materiality of the language it houses. Words in vertical proximity are separated at long last. The words "breathe," although they remain spatially linked in the alphabet, as well as in the poem by the poet's beautifully sly use of alliteration. The scents of the words in a sense linger along the liquid *l*'s, coalesce around the plucky *k*'s, wafting up as the book is opened. No human opener of the book is identified, although she hovers at the poem's margins, for it's the words themselves that have come alive in this poem.

If the poetry's music tethers Hutchins's poems internally, what holds them together in theme and subject is the thread of the elegiac at both personal and historical levels. First, there's memorialization of the cultured father descending into an Alzheimeric condition in which he still knows his wife and adult daughter, but not himself. "*Who's that?*" he's asked. "Oh! That's that smart man!" he responds ("Unrepeatable Poem"). Later, lines from Handel's magnificent *Messiah* will apply literally, tragically, to the father: "*we shall all be changed*" (as quoted in "We Shall All Be Changed"). Buried childhood memories surface as well, forging connections to traumatic history condensed metonymically into image and Imago, as in "The Resurfacing of Solano Avenue at the Millennium." The earth mover used to resurface the speaker's street reminds her of seeing *Night in Fog* when she was ten, of watching not earth but *human beings* "tractored." "Who can bear history?"

Hutchins asks hauntingly throughout this volume. But she refrains from simplifying the "unrepeatable," and in the familial and historical reckonings, Hutchins urges us not only to bear history, but to bear witness to it:

> At Auschwitz I placed my two hands flat on the gas
> chamber's wall, then flat on a brick oven's sliding drawer[.]
> . . . . When my hands flew
> to the roof of the mouth, like one blind I felt my way
> to where I had never been. I needed to trace the arch.
> To know what? Evil, and something more. . . .
>
> —"A Traveler Is Met by Touch"

That "something more" seems, at times, a moral imperative (to *imagine* evil, as Robert Duncan famously urged of Denise Levertov), but at other times in *Tender the Maker*, it is Life's unrepeatable, glorious Mystery, on which this beautiful collection so tenderly muses.

Cynthia Hogue

TENDER THE MAKER

One who is like a fountain flowing from itself
realizes her essence, and, passed through that motion,
bright creation—jubilant!—often closes with a beginning
and opens with an ending.

—Rainer Maria Rilke, *Sonnets to Orpheus* II.xii

Death is an accomplice of creation . . .
It is unanimous life: what gathers
and what disperses.

—Edmond Jabès, *From the Book to the Book*

ONE
World Without

INTERREGNUM

I was born wizened. Rasp of first breath,
I took the tinders of my parents' gazes and flinted
a honeyed flame. Before knowledge of cake or wood,

before even I was plated with a name, there were
cracklings and pleasings, wetly offered smiles and gasps:
I was old.

I took my place, and a heat
leapt up. Not mine,
but I tended it.

Drinklings, we are born to this necessity. To help. Helpless,
we snort the atmosphere, lunge toward milk, love. Eyes clouded,
lungs dewy with night, we emerge from the close cabin rocking

to a day already underway. Once I was emperor
of a body not my own, yet I craved the broken levee.
Haven, if it is haven, gives.

The swimmer passes
her piped body toward
the sting of light.

Ever after, the tear ducts remember. There was a beach
belonged to my mother's and my father's Sundays. We walked there.
Sometimes I was between them, holding both their young hands.

Then she turned old, and he was infirm,
rotting from within. I was the shunt of wreckage,
saffron-blue flame, versicolored

mermaid of the rocks,
fitted
for the abyss.

One by one, I took from my fingertips the limpet shells
I had worn like small roofs over touch. I stacked them, so many
tunics on the beach. My cinder cones.

Plum-hot the anvil, lava, the volcano's rise, ours
is a sky of yellow crumb and ash. Amorphous, still I am consuming,
yea and nay, and consumed,

but shaken loose: empress
of undertone, perilous foam,
creek in its natal dark.

BETWEEN PAGES OF THE DICTIONARY

Lift away *lurk* and let *lowbrow* breathe . . .
Language has lingered into slow scents: a library's
mottle-storming dust, cupcake breath,
inked leather. A luna moth left too long.

Nights so interminable can last years.
Cradled between *wheedle* and *wheel*,
watermark and *watchtower* wait in the dark.
Quietly bedded close, *wetnurse* went ahead:

she kisses *welterweight* without ceasing. Ever
breaching, *whale* meets *westerly* skin to skin,
and *wetly*, wetly (*damp, dank, moist*
in this desiccant dwelling) loves *well-worn*.

Worn well or by much use, o hackneyed thumb,
seek me, thin as water's moment
and still undefined. A shift has begotten
a transient beam. Quick, unload the seam.

ELEGY

Like some fall into the army,
the quick of commerce,
or whoredom, shield, the battlefield
soil, I fell

into the clear faces of a transposing
river. I woke to my father's
unprotected poverties, was schooled
by the slow

unbraidings of his dreams. I know
it is only luck to be unmistakably
loved. Affection bloomed,
trumpeting the hillsides,

the orchard valleys, and stopped
itself short of pillage. Guarded so,
vines suckled sun and drew winds
to the root.

Low clouds now, darkling a June
rain. A tender roof of tin.
I care. I am listening
for the fruit.

ATOP ZUGSPITZE

Sway of the tram
swung through my atlas of small bones,
at three I came to myself above the summer
Alps. A rock face loomed,

                         fell away,
and the first cable tower slid by,
grinding its dark gears.
Pressed between tall, sunlit brothers,

a window to the floor, I gathered the dreaming
folds of earth, shadow that I was.
Surge and dip beyond the tower, then another
                         another

                         and another,
silence between towers:
for years I dreamt the passage
through the soles of my feet.

How wind commanded and the tram rocked,
how a passing yellow gondola grasping
the down-running cable glided close
then sunk,

how three towers above the next notched
pass, from two black threads become one,
a miniature tram dangled
red then disappeared.

Atop Zugspitze, we each stepped out, Alpine
earth bared to early summer air. Brindle of snow
field, scent of sublimation, my father's
wide palm: he will live forever.

My mother, too, let go, even the clasp
of gender. It was Tante Gunhild, nearly
a stranger, who lifted me to the top rail, Gunhild
holding my coat, lightly and from behind.

Boots on the guardrail, I spread my arms:
the mountain cast away from its own
terrible boulders. An unbridled wind arose.

                                              I leaned into

the mouth of my making.

DIE ROTE JACKE

A mother with a painter's eye
dressed the shy child
to run red among the stones

Gray building stones and fountain stones—
slipped from mother and father among
the brown cobble of village streets
black of brick and the upshiftings
of Alpen peaks

the red coat announced
what the voice could not—
Ich bin Gegensatz und Feuer
I am contrast
and bright fire

Warmes und fliessendes Blut habe ich
I am blood   warm
flowing among the winter-damp stones
Fanget!
Ich bin Blumenblatt:

Catch!
Take both my hands
and swing between you
the brush-stroke   a flung petal
caught—

your mother would like
I think your mother   a red sweater
something a trip   a boat the three of us

Afternoon listing across the same never-
before room   he and I sat in the memory-care
unit   leaned close on a couch

and I rested my head
on his shoulder   riding
wherever we went

Yes!   Your mother
We'll do that yes for her
Voice who sang me through the early waters

and still tuning my intricate ear
How will world be
world without?

Don't you think
                          Your mother

would

MY BROTHERS

Later of course they turned nasty.
Tim pinned me to the hardwood floor,
    let spit   dangle   over my face,

        sucking it back in
                just in time
or not.

One Christmas Day, Dave
engraved our father's new record set,
                Die Schöpfung,

        hard-pressed a pencil,
my name in my five-year-old scrawl.
Laughing, he watched me punished.

        But before the world leaned into its light
and its shadow, they were there in a colorless dark
                holding my hands.

        (In the beginning the earth was
        a formless void, and darkness
        covered the face of the deep.)

I walked between them,
our six boots on wooden sidewalks
                above the snow.

        (Es war einmal im Märchenwald.
        Das Welt war grau, und alles
        war dunkel und still.)

To me they were half-giants striding
among shuttered clouds. Later
    of course they turned,

    but once upon time itself my brothers,
confident of where we were going,
clasped my hands

and tread slowly. I was
not abandoned before the unmade
   nor left alone

in the terror of making.
       Already departing from the past,
             our boot-heels became the flung

voices of silent boards:
             rhythmic prophesies,
                    first colors sounding a world

     regenerate, not new,
for the old, resonant grain was haven
to sapling traces of green.

OUR PASSING

Be the motion of flame by which a memory is reignited
in the splendor of its change and escapes from you . . .
—Rainer Maria Rilke, *Sonnets to Orpheus* II.xii

At the foot of a two thousand year-old redwood
someone bends down to me, but I strain against
the bar of a stroller toward you, eye of the camera,
memory before mine. Henry Cowell State Park

Memorial Grove, the afternoon of the first
step of so many, leaning forward, trusting earth
and my own muscled leg, not just to catch
but to further me, near the place, I slow.

Driving Highway 9 past Felton, flood barricades
block the night road, and the bridge out,
I turn back. Behind these trees looms
a life kindled early, this night

dark as when we crowded the charred hollow,
the General Fremont Tree. There is a bench here.
Feel your way to it. Sit beside me.
I will hold your hand

so the flash won't startle you. Your palm wide,
smooth as it ever was, I am ten,
we have walked down to the river where afternoon
sun heats dragonflies to blue flames.

Take my hand. The bank is steep here.
I have unlaced my boots, left them on the edge of the road.
The yellow soil slips, and my feet learn to grip like hands.
Here is what I know: you wanted my joy,

the pleasures of my feet on cold stones, clear
water of the San Lorenzo early summer. You wanted
my hair escaping its braids, my pantlegs rolled wet
and unrolled in the car. You wanted my hands

on the picnic basket well before lunch, my sandy
feet on the blanket, my voice under douglas fir
taking up the air. You wanted my tired head
dropped against the vinyl seat behind you as you drove

Highway 17, taking the curves, heading home, the sun
keening orange in your rearview mirror—while alongside us
the laurel oaks, the bays and redwoods and cedars
cheered our passing with deep evening boughs.

ASYLUM

(under nearly every uttered or: the right and)

A near riot at the garden plot: every bloom
shingles a seed. Sweet alyssum, each scent's
guarding something sly, a neverbefore.

Close the trap and slam fast the gate. Toss
the code to the dawn. Though language
has obscured the playground, its borders can be

breached: stints and stones, bars, railing,
chain-link, grave. Just try me. Grasp it. Under
nearly every shuttered door: the bright hand.

THE MUSIC INSIDE

As early morning I stood high on a kitchen chair,
firm hands unbraided, brushed, and damp-braided
my hair. The barrette clasped tight, my mother rough-
pulled her comb through my brush. I trotted

a cloud of childhair out to the yard,
laid it on the tips of the grass. First rays arrested
among the flutes and stems, scent of a darkwater birth,
this is the dew inside the dew.

This is the truck inside the truck, the plane
inside the airplane I drew early most afternoons,
a psychological puzzle handed over to my mother.
This is the poem inside the poem.

Late in the day, polished boards streamed light
under a closet door locked from without. Half an inch
seeping through every luminescent leaf, lemonade
stand, white wicker, and Kimberly-pink child nipple,

this is the child inside the child, cross-legged
below the brush of coat hems. Beside the bright stripe
on the dark of the neighbor's floor, silence was thickening
to song. Released at suppertime, I jogged home

past crowds of juniper thorn and poison peas,
chest-high clappers of the bell that was my outstretched
arm, my round and rosined palm. "Ring," I said.
I sang, "wrangle, wrung."

Amid the bell-towers of sycamore and birch, a high
wind rose and rang every tongue of garrulous green.
Fists of first drops, fragrant the breath
of tarp and tarmac, a hidden creek rattled.

A joyful dog barked the letters of foul words.
A piebald horse took a weed-lined walk.
A mower and a mower's own path following it,
all of us grew damp and damper:

The cantering horse. The joyful dog.
Bright the shorn. Stubble. The creek!
This is the drummed bottom of a blue plastic pool,
empty, upended.

Hairs, collected and abandoned, line the inner nests
of unknown birds. I left the cage door open while I slept.
Dank as an albatross and happy at the flute hotel,
I fastened the past with a loose clasp.

TWO

A Day Already Underway

> *There is being sifted*
> *The sand of your time, turning as you turn . . .*
> *Some day, not accountable, you may look down*
> *To see in your palm as on a field of history*
> *The grain of time you recognize as yours.*

— Josephine Miles, "Toward II" in *To All Appearances*

EYE OF THE STORM, PESCADERO COAST, 1972

The same shirt pulled over the same head
not once but again and again, a eucalyptus turned
inside out. Brutal, foam-white,

the sea tore at its rocky coast. Route One was
forsaken. The big house was unlit, the plowed yard
a pool of rain. A cloud ceiling

pressed yet lower. Along worn cliffs
in the farm workers' small-windowed shacks, stoves
burned into the dark of the day.

It was Sunday, but only the storm made it
Sabbath. In flooded fields, unharvested
Brussels sprouts clung to their stalks.

EMBERS OF THE DAY

For years I waited with eucalyptus
       through oncoming dark
   as slope by slope
     was lit

            and extinguished—
last spark and breath of the day
A sky no longer fierce
      rose and topaz dulled to spelter ash

Whole hillsides of redwood and laurel oak
            faded and folded down rustling
    a massive chorus section by section
settling into silence

But eucalyptus' papery bark and silver leaves
     still craved a remainder of daylight
        the dry-canyoned stir
of a wanton afternoon

     and though the surrounding world
    had already pledged its hours
to the night
and to stillness

one by one
   narrow and pale as our long bones
each abiding tree   chosen and blown upon
      began to glow—

I was eyes and ears of the forest
as out of the bellowed dark
       each form
         loomed

whispering sinew and amber
and leaning its trembling length toward me
       chanced
          a slender step—

CLEANING OUT THE GARAGE IN 1968

we found Alexander the Salamander
slick orange and black-spotted
and missing for months
    flattened into a dry membrane
under the worn cardboard Allied

Vanlines box where spiders wove
together the giant sweet-smelling
      fingers of baseball gloves
where we dumped the basketball
to rest in shadows beside the ticking

engine cooling to silence
      the ball still hot
from its driveway *poing poing*   still
damp from our palms   where under
the football   wooden bat   warped

Frisbee and a zippered Lufthansa bag
a badminton net lay tangled
in itself   So many years ago
I learned this dread of your death—
    a lifetime of dread—

Beams of the day reached into the garage
   and struck an already brittling stack
of newspapers where Dr. King
      still marched   I was seven years old
It was the newspapers   The dusted sunlight

It was Alexander's desiccated body
pressed thin as a ping-pong paddle
    translucent as apricots held to the sun
        and it was an old shoe
dried into the same stiffness

laces untied and dangling and
shadow where your foot should be
    the leather tongue
still molded to the known
curve of your high instep

THE RESURFACING OF SOLANO AVENUE AT THE MILLENNIUM

i.

Gravel and dust   the pavement gone
each belled shop-door was still propped open
Solano Avenue was fragmented—
chunks of sub-road and old pipe

like monuments lifted then shoved aside
Incandescence stretched
onto a lavender roadbed   rumpled
as if by earthquake or by war

Earthmovers
        crouched in the dusk
    Their massive claws silent   were clamped
            and curled inward

ii.

Who can bear history?
                        Each living child
            sits beneath the foundations
upon which her necessary world assembles

iii.

I would have liked to drive one
roll unstoppable
    raise the scooping
        arm   high   *high*—

iv.

        but the year I turned ten
                    there was *Night In Fog*—
From 8mm had tumbled the tractored *human beings*
and still the train

v.

            slowing to pass through
warehouses and intersections
       will not quit sounding
    its unyielding   irresolvable chord

I plied my way—   Like a dry riverbed
there was another street below the ruined street
Calm with dusk   air coolly lifted
chalky musk   old concrete crumbling

and sifted by smell   the adult earth rolled open
became Karlsruhe 1964   concrete dust
before the pour   where brand-new houses
are lifting daily and deserted late each afternoon

Yellow wood and brown beer bottles
half empty   sand in shovel-stripped piles drenched gray
alive in an unutterable world   still I breathe
the mute meetings of making and decay—

vi.

For before cement was mixed or dumped
       scraped or troweled or set   I too
   sat on the scrabbled earth
         under houses and graves

                  Under road and river
    I played—
turning small subterranean
      stones in a child's bare palm

O SUN, 2003

No, No, thou which since yesterday hast been
Almost about the whole world, hast thou seen . . .
O sun, in all thy journey, vanity
Such as swells the bladder of our court?

—John Donne, "Satire 4"

O sun, you remember percussion and pause.
Through charred undergrowth and the unleafed
jungle near a sieved village, decades ago you
illumined two soldiers, their faces: one was Lifeless
and the other Agony. The bodily-alive cradled
his beloved, dead, and in stark black and white
you pressed light into death,
until by its image we were changed.

Now, like soap bubbles the practice balls ascend
and soar, then fall. Under them, teenagers
weave the far field, their bodies lithe
and whole. You green the mid-March grass!
Shouldering a sea of air, you ride
the balls' unhurried arcs. I can hear a distant
percussion and pause, but it is just
a foot, only a soccer ball rising,

lashed to the gravity that draws it home.
Sun, landing among the eager blades of earth,
Which mortals dare dictate human grief?
Tell the tin roof their specious names.
Exact the spectrum of truths. Strike
the slanted window, the chrome: angle
unstinting, and scream away. Stain
every retina—even the closed eye—

HUMPTY IN OUR HANDS

i.

I was part sky. From a height of seven metres, my songs
rained into the village. From eight royal yards, my baritone
cascaded the castle. I watched the world
to its visible edge.

From both sides of the wall I was known. Some days
I faced one way, some the other. Flinging my legs
over the width, with the momentum I spun on my axis
to dangle on the sunny side,

and the far side became this side, these faces.
I longed for touch. Twenty-four blackbirds once
perched close, yellow feet clung rough to the stones.
Almost, I could stroke their fiery backs—

When they drifted down to yank castle yardworms
from the morning grass, a maid snatched them
one by one with bare hands. The king was
in the counting house. Those birds,

they would not stop. Their voices rang round and
round my head. I wanted to last like that.
As they sifted down the light, their coal-black wings
flashed crimson—   Once,

ii.

I stood up on my thin, blue legs. On heels made for lightly
banging the shins of rocks, I placed the weight of my own
becoming. Balanced on a parapet,
cool stone succored the soles of my feet.

Glimpsing my face in the moat, so tiny, so far from
myself and clear (a windless day, the water neither
ruffled nor whispered), maybe I wanted what I saw.
Maybe it was that day I leaned too—

iii.

Or. Maybe it was the day I saw a woman reading a book.
Like the courtyard sun over her shoulder, through
the intervening air, I read with her. Her musical fingers
flipped quiet paper. Like a drawn curtain, a shadow

slid over, and the text disappeared. The shadow solid,
her own soft shoulder, her wild head—I wanted to turn
the page. Her body alongside mine. Wanted
red-flecked wings—

iv.

Or was it that humid day and my glasses. Without them
I can't see the roofs of the barns. My glasses, first reach
when I wake. Moisture, breath, rubbing them to clarity,
when they leapt from my grasp, I lunged after—

v.

I didn't really believe death. I knew so little of effort,
my own or anyone else's. Was love an array, the pieces I saw
from my wall? Gangs of birds, servants through the scullery
window, broken leaves walking this way and that,

bunching in purgatory corners and floating
yellow flags on moat's dark. Fragment and trajectory,
unavoidable dissolution was everywhere. The wall was dusty
in the flat places. My knees began to ache.

In the moat, water snakes
rose and thrashed. In the kitchen,
cook cracked an egg.

The metal rim of the mixing bowl rang a joy knell—
Was it then?   Or. That other time, answering a letter.
At the crucial word, my pen ran out of ink. I reached for
the borrowed one, handed up with a pole, and—

The fork ran away with the
spoon,   and Mr. Humpty gained
his second name.   The wheelbarrow,

scoop,   the bin.   All night
we worked and to no avail.   I lost
my taste for shatterings.

A shard in my pocket,
I dared leave
        the king's army.

vi.

Swinging, I was swinging my feet. Maybe it was
laughter that made me. Careless. Or rage. Maybe determined,
I flung myself down. Maybe it was all procrastination and
I should have let go long ago—

The horses' hooves. Too much,
the clatter. But those sad, gentle soldiers,
all their hands!

FROM THE HOLD

Desolate these days and beyond, set loose
from their use in any imaginable world.
Tingling of distal limbs, every bird
is a blade sharpening on the stones,

and the skull so shrill-packed, such a ship
set sail, of course it will sink or explode:
the old infant seams, their ancient seals,
bone plates adrift in time.

What pent cargo could require a silence
so exacting? Wood pronged loose
from a feathered joint, harbored continents
spread from their assumed moorings.

Corpses of a boiling sea, survivors
cling to flotsam. How dare we go there
in our tidy boats full of clean towels. How dare
the ordinary be brutal and needing us.

Red and bristol blue is survival: its first joy
and its lasting reflections. The life-filled boats
are rowed through molten colors.
Some of the ferried can laugh.

Some moan. Some trail their hands
through a clear, receptive water gone sweet,
on whose passive tensions we proceed
finally and mostly together.

UNREPEATABLE POEM

i.

Last rainy day on the trail, a man fitness-walking
as we plodded, asked, *What are you doing out here?*
"We're out here to laugh," my father said.

ii.

On the porch-swing, he and I lean together.   *How many
fingers am I holding up?* "Seventy." *What time
is it?* "Seventy-one."

In McDonalds, his soda spilled, root beer dripping
everywhere—his chest, his lap, the curved plastic
seat, the floor—   "What was that explosion?"

His voice again, a desperate sundown,   "They're locked.
It's terrible. They're all locked in." *Are you
lonely?* "Yes."

A hot August day and a slow walk, both thick-soled
beige shoes dragging. He stops to point at
his feet.   "I've got chairs on those."

Last photo of the three of us, he picks out my mother
and me. She points to the one he doesn't name,
Who's that?   "Oh! That's that smart man!"

iii.

Weaving the nearly empty hall,   "Dots are going past
my eyes." After a hospital night we hold onto him
from both sides. His heart is fibrillating.

"There are Creatures."   Getting a shave, he is grimacing
and happy. *Are there some creatures you like?*
"The kind of creatures that keep their distance!"

iv.

Walking around the outside of the locked unit,
he studies the wall.   "We should paint it."   *What color
would you like to paint it?*   "Light water."

v.

                A nursing assistant approaching
the dayroom smiles at him.   "There's the one
with the beautiful hole in her face."

Beethoven's *Pathetique*, the Adagio.   Groaning, he
hugs the piano.   "When you put out your—"   he pounds
his breastbone.   *Music?*   "*Yes!* Then I find myself."

Alive in the moving air. He in the middle,
my mother and he and I on the porch-swing rocking so high
one of the chains comes loose.

The hospice therapist.   *How does the music make you
feel?*   "Sad."   *What are you sad about?*   "When you have to be
some place, and you can't get out."

THE DISAPPEARING DOORS

Don't despair if you begin in joy,
the day still new on its hinges,
and end at evening distraught,
all that radiant air and easy access
gone, the day shut up tight
and painted closed.

O celebration, human, do not despair the days,
your life. In Venice, old stone stairs
march down the tide. Slow-rising
waters submerge the generations, remnant
hollows of their footsteps, cupped sills,
the houses' bright doors.

Below the glittering underside of the surface
of the sea sways a dark-gemmed world. Fish dart;
long-stemmed weeds undulate. A storied
incandescence ceaselessly rocks.
The doors, when they open,
must open to those tides.

THREE
Haven, If It Is Haven, Gives

Every glad aperture is a child or grandchild of a parting
through which pass the astounded . . .
 —Rainer Maria Rilke, *Sonnets to Orpheous* II.xii

QUAIL

The roof's edge. A quiet touch of cool,
intimate air. A quail's voice, scrabbling dawn
from the undersides of berry leaves: the screen
lets pass what is without

and light, and brightening. The screen lets pass
what is within and too dense to be contained.
My brother has opened the window.
Nothing more can be lost here.

A small family of quail strides out for seed
spilled from an old man's hand. Later today
it will be winter rain in spring, but
this is seed left over, spread out

for the bobbing quail yesterday afternoon
when even Beethoven failed,
when Newell, having dragged a plastic
patio chair into the Saturday sun and tidily

crossed his trousered legs, dozed
in two right shoes—one white one black—
when Helen, walking her wheelchair along
with quick shuffling feet,

came again and again to the closed room
across the hall and knocked at her own door—
when beyond all tenderness
the surf of breath rose and thrashed,

and we thought that ocean never would
settle, or still, or cease its jailed burning,
until just before first light,
first bird, he did cease.

(California, 1960)

birch light traveled around our heads, our arms,
down your father's back. I knew the instant you
were in me: how it was you, who
you were and yet as always a stranger
more unbecome than become.

You were a wanted child.
We sent your brothers to their room
for an afternoon nap.

They went so easily—as if remembering something
or willing it. Dave climbed the ladder,
and Tim lay down on the bottom bunk.
Always restless, David's jutting legs
lay quiet. Tim had that half-smile he used to get.

By the time I pulled their drape,
both boys were asleep. Just before,
I had stood with the knotted

cord in my hand. It was August, the window
open. Wind was rattling the soft coins of plum leaf.
I knew the empty corner of the garden
would take to pansies and alyssum.
By the time my hand was on the doorknob,

the drape was billowing and retreating, swelling
into the room and flinging itself back
flat against the screen: a sucked, suckling thing.

That summer afternoon everything sought to be
skin to skin. The pull-cord thwacked the wall,
a small staccato
counterpoint to the breath-rhythms.
When I closed the bedroom door, I turned

into your father's two hands around my waist,
into our singular hour. Birch shadows set
a moving grain to every still thing.

VIGIL

*We watched as a man came
and took away the body
to be burned.*

Shut for all
the days of my
father's dying

in death
his left lid
would not stay closed

but opened alone
Wider than life
the blue eye

gazed unflinching
directly at my mother
and me and my brother

who groaned
a sob and turned
his face into

my chest where
I shielded him
not at all

i.

Not me turning the corner but what
comes. At Sequoia we ate at a rough
wood table on a little rented porch.
Day after day, my brothers and
my father, too, teased,

Chris, there's a bear. It's coming
around the corner! I was eight and tired
of being duped. Corn on the cob, butter
melts between kernels, again
the warning tumbles

from their busy mouths. They gather
plates, the salad bowl, their cups of milk,
they cross the planks and insist. Even
my mother goes. They shut the cabin
door. Steadfast, I savor my corn.

A bear, her shifting shoulders, her
fur rust-red in late slats of sun, comes
round the corner of the porch. Two
black cubs lingering behind her,
she starts up the wooden

stair. I am on my feet. Face
to face, now, she and I. Her head is
huge. Her breath sweet, she is here:
the truth after lies. From the little
rented cabin a great clatter

begins. The cubs scoot up
a vertical tree. I hear their claws sink
deep in the thick, soft bark. She
looks at me. I look
at her. I could touch

her, but I don't. We turn away.
Did she back down the wooden
steps, return the way she came? I'm
across the porch without touching
feet to the floor. I'm

through the door that was
opened to me. In the dust-mote
dusk of the cabin, my mother, banging
an upturned garbage can, my brother
with pot-bottom and spoon,

I am in my father's arms.
I'm sorry. I am in his voice. *I'm
sorry.* The voice blooms in the dark.
*We should not have teased you
like that.*

ii.

Not them but me and what
comes too fast. I was mid-thirties
and ready to be a child. Waterside
of the tracks north of Richmond,
San Francisco's swells

become San Pablo Bay, and short,
orange cliffs undulate with blue.
My lover then, she was an explorer.
We wandered alone in the surprising
wilderness between

desolate cities. We walked the tracks.
Creosote and gravel, we balanced
the beams of the rails. I prized steel
through the soles of my shoes, and the land
turned away from the sea.

Bright the curving rails, shining
to near a single point, while far away,
slow on another twist of meager land, a train
tiny and black draws a thin line of smoke.
The lover ran

down the embankment. I dug
a penny from my pocket. A bit of lint
drifted, languid, and the distant train
disappeared. The cliffs were so
quiet. I bent and set

the penny on the rail: copper
the afternoon, copper the cliffs,
the stones, copper the tiny specks
of rust dusting the steel of the rail!
Thunder black the train

around the bend bearing down
close as my soul and all momentum.
Huge, the engine: white-hot the sun,
center of its face. What looms, here
and louder than my life? I ran or rolled,

did I? The horn, sounding the rage
of the engineer. Iron weight of a horse furious
on earth, thrashing away. The bay, lapping.
Stupid! The lover was crying. *That was such
a stupid thing to do.*

iii.

Everywhere, I am finding pennies.
Spangling sidewalks, countertops,
the podium, the ledge. My father,
each time he opened the change snap
of his black wallet,

reached in with the thick index
finger and thumb of his left hand and
plucked me a penny from his purse.
For five days, six nights, he
breathed hard as a runner

sucking air. Then pause, pause
a full minute between the seven rolling breaths
like waves. My brother and I, we nested him
best we could. The rattling, and, at last,
those tiny peaceful breaths,

breath so slight it nourished nothing
but the spirit. He had labored.
Dying, he labored to turn the corner,
but it was not my father
that turned.

When the quiet finally came,
there was no breath in him.
He lay curled as we had pillowed him,
before and behind, his broad forehead
a rock-face I kissed.

Like sleep, like a dream,
it came of its own. Perhaps it
filled the room. At this place
my words are labored as his
breath. What comes

around the corner comes not
by footsteps or on heavy wheels but
weightless and irrevocable—how he curls
in the memory that is
my own body—

and I cannot, nor
would I if I could, leap
away from the silent
confrontation that comes
amid the clatter.

PASSING THROUGH THE APERTURE

for my mother and my brother, Tim

An underwater swimmer
mantled with bubbles
let go fraught worlds.

They globed syllabic and silver.
What green bird rose
dripping from that damped

fire? If our sleep channeled
the birth, what purpled
mouth bore him?

Wake up. He's gone.

The child
held the crackle in her hand,
became something she'd never been.

It was a good fortune: open-ended, fitted,
specific. Read once, twice, it kept curling
to the shape that had cradled it.

A shadow prison burst, the tablecloth's
full of leavings: crumbs and strewn utensils,
empty tea-cups,

the apostrophe she wakes into
each morning.

FOUR
Plum-Hot the Anvil

Survival is a matter of avowing a trace of loss
that inaugurates one's own emergence.
 —Judith Butler, *The Psychic Life of Power*

I woke in the dusk of dawn to a small jubilation,
orange juice filling a glass. Strike of a match,
metal-to-metal twist of the key, sputter and flow
of white-gas, without seeing I saw my father
pumping the Coleman stove, the valve-spun ease

of his thick thumb on the steel piston, the ring of fire.
I listened, eyes still closed, to the diction of the creek,
raised loud by night air and just begun its decrescendo, the slip
into daylight and disappear. Cold on my face, damp canvas,
my body was warm, and the day before arrived again:

the spigot beside campsite number nine, eager *chug-chug*
of water finding the canteen, the pot, the gathered stones
at the base and exceeding them, leaping a little, a spritz
of mud on one shin. Scent of ancient flannel, the past
ever before me hones the tone of a coming day.

I breathed and heard again the magician, the fire-maker,
my father lifting a spatula from the utensil box
percussion. Tent poles in both hands,
he had lifted his arms, and with his arms, the great
blue tent, tongue between his right incisors,

just the tip curled in view. "You'll bite it off someday,"
my mother warned. And under the low rail-trestle, late
afternoon, my feet in a water-strider creek, cool
the cadence, the confiding stones, *My cape is leaves of air,*
I sang. *My feet are shod with water.*

Later, the dish-tub set on a wet wooden bench, both arms
plunged in and streaked with shine, small jet of a lantern,
popcorn escaped the pot, and kernels opened everywhere,
little fireworks on the picnic table, white on the night-
sky of the ground. Creek stones, hoarded as jewels

and bound to dry, sat dull as the rocks by the road.
My mother turning cards on the tablecloth's faded flowers,
slapping the faces down, I fell into sleep to voices in air
and the silent pauses, double solitaire. My father
cleared his throat. An opera singer, baritone,

sometimes he laughed Mephistopheles' laugh, drawn long
and sliding down the scale of evil. I lifted the tent-flap
to a wetted world: it was dew. The refiner.
Clothier of the grass, the bottleglass tinker of stones.
The music that wracks and sustains a life moves

by appoggiatura, notes that require, drive resolution:
the *Adagietto* of Mahler's 5th. Early in the Alzheimer's,
my father would pocket any key, and we took to hiding
keys and pocket-change. Then Mephistopheles began to laugh:
in the surgical waiting room, walking the produce aisles.

His body shook with song: *The trumpet shall sound
and the dead shall be raised incorruptible.* The voice remained,
but the words began to slip. *If God so clothe
the grass of the fields, will she not, will we not, much more
clothe you? O, ye of little faith.*

When I emerged from the tent, the azure flame was steady.
I tell you a mystery: we shall all be changed.
Even losing himself, even lost, my father
woke to a past retold by its worth. I tell you
a mystery—our past is change and will change me—

in the twinkling of an eye. Steady, the blue ring of fire
was flit with gold: small darts and trumpet-flares,
bright orange salamanders of the cave. There are sadnesses
that travel permanently, the gem collector's bitter
citrus, shot through with first embers of sun.

RESERVOIR AT UVAS CANYON

It was my parents' canoe,
but for a few late summer afternoons
I owned the rolling column of water
beneath it. I knelt barefoot

in rolled up pants, damp with featherings
of an ash paddle lifted across the boat,
entering the water one side awhile,
then the other, every now

and then banging the aluminum side.
A big, lit drum, we reverberated clear
down through gem green, down
into the buried dark, pressed

and pressing cold, wall to unforgiving wall.
The air dry and roots exposed, almost
forgotten were the rains. The spillway loomed
high overhead: we floated

under its concrete mouth. Ankles
sloshing, we dragged the boat partway up
a yellow-soil bank and scrambled up the listing
stone to sit on the great lip.

Dangling our legs, my friend and I
ate pork and beans from the can
with a single plastic spoon. We did not
litter. We did not sing.

When light, having tutored us
in traces of loss, yielded its final radiance,
the captive water deepened. We chilled
at the growing expanse, cradled and pent

against the earthen dam beneath us,
until, relentless, the hundred years' flood
rose to gallop through our own
precarious, balancing bodies.

FIVE
Accomplice of Creation

*There is nothing which belongs merely to the privacy
of feeling of one individual . . . All origination is private.
But what has been thus originated, publicly pervades
the world.*

—Alfred North Whitehead, *Process and Reality*

DEPARTURE

a station.
a station growing smaller and smaller.
a moment ago there was a station.

to touch the excess of departure,
she had plunged her hands
into the fountains of Karlsruhe.

no longer two become a distant one,
shining, the liquid rails
splay.

The beautiful stranger
became two, then more,
the way ice, melting,
finally breaks from itself,

and, with unforgeable
signatures, the pieces
free the river. I lay flat
on the rush of a stranger's

body. Have splayed
to hear shuttered spirits
shift and groan below
a winter-lidded lake.

In Gdansk where the mouths
of Wislaw and Motlawa
find the Baltic, the gates
of the shipyards stand

open. Miroslaw, you
were there that spring, when
after a winter of martial
law, the river-

ice began to pile
high as it does every
spring. But how inexorable
it was! Each

heaped and still frozen
boulder had become
a changing face, a public
notice, wet with tears.

LINSEED

Through my mother's jars fell the light of plums.
At Capistrano the swallows returned. I loved
the bitter scent of linseed, crumbs of pigment,
& while she painted, dragged my child-fingers

lightly along adobe walls. Once I swung
on the high gate of a graveyard. It opened
a carnival of death: crooked stones & violate
grasses, broken fence, sunken shibboleth.

Breath marries the quiet beats of a wing.
A bird evades her oils. Geranium
under the arch, red, red, & ding-a-ling
sway in the wind, glide & rise on the thrum.

Who knew at Auschwitz the grass would be
so very green? The barbs were thickets
of thorns all in a row. One summer day
I stood, adult, in the hygiene chamber.

From the low doorway it darted,
a shadow. It slid into the concrete
wall. It was a small cleft,
her nest, dark swallow, her red eye.

A TRAVELER IS MET BY TOUCH

A cinder never quite burned out.
—René Char, The Formal Share

In St. Petersburg I leaned into garden air and from Anna
Akhmatova's windowsill took up a greening breeze.
When I turned the spigot of her samovar, nothing visible
poured. I tried on her father's winter coat.

In Krakow a Bösendorfer fell under my fingers. In Salzburg
I lost my nametag. On both my watches the same sweep,
though one was billow and the other gamble: I dared caress
an acrobat. I learned a pulse, stroked a shaven head.

At Auschwitz I placed my two hands flat on the gas
chamber's wall, then flat on a brick oven's sliding drawer,
a raft so narrow on its tempered rails. When my hands flew
to the roof of the mouth, like one blind I felt my way

to where I had never been. I needed to trace the arch.
To know what? Evil, and something more. To follow the path
of risen smoke? Last year my father was incinerated,
a tag on his memorized toe. His ash

scattered by strangers beyond the Golden Gate, it was
weeks later I plunged my arms into the Bay, into an arriving
tide, surges of water under the Bridge.
Finally nearing home again, I discover a sprinkler

spinning and tacking, flushing a granite-dry earth
into its greenly darkening duff. The glittering load
sets itself down here and here, and here, until every blade
of our small topography, sated, releases drop

by drop its accumulated burden of gifts, mercuric
and sliding edge to edge. From the immensity of Birkenau
I stole a fingernail of brick. Spark of the ruined chamber,
the need to touch and be touched again.

LARK

Can you make a poem about this? About us.
—M. P.

Like me, you are descended from
royalty, no matter how thin the line
of rabbis, esteemed mayors of the old
city. Great grandchild of the tiger
lily, the Polish Pope's second
cousin once removed, or, like me,
some bubble of high seas blown along
the Mayflower's deck,

you, too, are of the undertow:
tired mothers' lithe fingers, ditch-labors
of fathers, the crouched lover, a school-
yard friend whispering rebellion
through the slats. Clandestine blooms,
hidden birds of the field, neither
did they spin themselves
fictions of the crest.

Slipped amid root stems
of the venerable grain, tiny daisies
sustain the earth. The found
is so small: tomorrow's enfolded
alteration and the memory of my hands
around your close-shorn head. Quick,
the acclaimed swallow falls
silent. But bunting, sparrow,

what is that other bird,
the shy one who tucks both
wings to its sides mid-flight
to sing? Tight little body-plummet
between wing-beats. This morning
your name rests so bright
on my tongue. Yes, Miroslaw,
the folded moment can be sung.

BEING READ

We aren't the only readers. While mist studies
the shower door, clear drops page down your skin.
Shape-notes in a stream, we're clung by curiosity.

Packed sands memorize undulating shapes of the sea;
grasses spell out a grainy sun. Steep a second
cup of tea. While architects

erase the firmament, ducks in waddle-lines
jam the riverbanks and pray. There is so much ardor
under ink. Behind my mother's house, toads'

two-toned voices massage the air. Sometimes the same
rains stalk several bookshops: the toads' sepia skins,
a tin cup full of creek, our ladled thirsts.

CONFESSIONS OF A TACTILE KLEPTOMANIAC

On an island in the Mirabel Palace garden live thirteen stone dwarves
not counting the two guarding the footbridge.
The third from the right looks like my father.

Though I have left wishes everywhere (with a penny in the eye
of the Kapuzinerberg wall, I turned around the pivot of the turning
world), there are things I have stolen,

some with great shame. Pink granite from the walkways of Peterhof,
quartz from the sugarpaths of Catherine the Great. A soft little stone
from an Auschwitz lane. My father's glasses, smudged with the final salt.

Five cherry tomatoes disappeared from the blue bowl when no one was in the room.
Thighs of a lover, a mouth. Stowed in my pocket, a petal from the garland
of Milosz' marble tomb. There is nothing abstract about my hands.

When I was finally left alone with them, the dwarves began to move.
Pockmarked and frangible, sly, they. Ever so softly shifting positions
without shifting positions, the things people do when alone.

Drinking from the spigot. Mumbling eeny meeny miney moe.
Blowing up balloons and letting them go, grand elocutions: rescuing a dead
starfish by tossing it back to sea, arguing with the radio news, sniffing

an onion for the rush of tears. Eating from the fingers, from the fork upside down,
absently licking the blade of the knife. (If everyone pilfered as I do,
would there no longer be a world?) Sliver of railroad tie,

a blackened shard of Birkenau's chambers. The gaze of an icon during Orthodox
prayer. Krakow's high trumpet! The cheer of the crowd on the Stadtplatz,
it was a World Cup, the energy of thousands loosed on the air.

I do stow things, too: on a tiny path in Mozart's woods, flute shop
of *Die Zauberflöte*, I found a poem in multiple voices, and under a flat rock
I hid it. It named the names, took up a secret, public place.

From an upstairs window of the Mirabel Palace, Debussy rained
from the fingers of a Russian pianist. Higher than the patrons' patterned ceiling
arched the dusking sky. In the courtyard stood a man without arms,

looking up. He took it, the resonance of the courtyard walls, and so did I.
The rain was real. We drank and we bathed.
Our hair was wet when it ended.

From Mozart I learned one requiem is all that is required. The stone-bronze
dwarf in Mirabel's garden was lent the daemon-spirit of my father, his dying,
wild hair. The forehead loomed. It burned, and it cooled.

On each dwarf's body, I touched whatever protuberance or crevice
beckoned: tongue of the first, breast, cup of the hand. Bent nose,
terrible knot risen on the head, button, a swollen ear.

When I came to my father, I touched the temples, the familiar nose.
The garden had emptied. I touched the blank eyes. My lips
took the forehead I kissed while he died and was dead.

A WAY BACK TO LIFE

From Russians I learned never to shake hands
across a threshold, but a half-hour after
rising, I return to set my cool hand into the bed
where a river of dreamheat lingers, the still-warm
flank of our horse's dark gallop.

To make sure it was me they got, my parents
put up all night with a mockingbird
perched aloud in one of three liquid birches
a handspan from their open window. Do you
think I'd make that up? Ask me,

and I might tell you the joke that rolls
like a yellow marble from all that I have made.
A cloak of lightning around my shoulders,
I can slip like a drumbeat into the actual world.
If only making love did not

also make loss. If only a curtain call
and the dead lifted their bodies,
lithe. From the surprise taxi emerged a child
beautiful in her buttoned coat, but on the stones
even her small feet sang

the terrible clatter. You have suggested we
take the floating trip, meaning, perhaps, without
formal destination. Will you bury your head
in the softness of my belly where old
yearnings still sleep? Continent

to continent, homeless and without
fixed beliefs, perhaps a large part laughter,
there is nowhere loss will refuse
to take us. I have decided to trust
the late night horse and its riders.

The translations of the Rilke epigraphs from *Die Sonette an Orpheus, II.xii* are my own. The phrase "realizes her essence" can also be translated "recognizes herself as made by the making," so realizing one's "essence" is not discovering a preexistent, enduring self but the dynamic of the artist realizing self as a motion-in-relation through which the work of art completes itself. The work of art may be a poem or a conversation. It may be a human lifetime.

"Between Pages of the Dictionary." When a book is closed, each word spends a great deal of time in private intercourse with the word on a facing page. I cracked *Webster's Collegiate*, 10th Edition, just enough almost to catch them in the act.

"My Brothers." Italic sections are Genesis 1:1–2 and phrases that open a fairy tale: *Once upon a time in a forest . . . the world was gray, and everything was dark and quiet. Die Schöpfung* is Georg Frederick Handel's oratorio *The Creation*. The poem is set in 1964 West Germany, not far from the Black Forest.

"Asylum." Though "an ear riot at the garden plot" might prefer to keep its tiny, dark secrets, an *ars poetica* hides within the obvious poem. As in music, when a traceable motif resides within a larger melodic phrase, words exist within other words, and the latter can't be read without simultaneously reading the former. "Every loom hinges a see, each sense guarding a verb. Lose the rap and slam fast the gate. Toss the ode to the dawn . . . orders can be reached: tints and tone, ailing in ink. Just rhyme. Rasp it. Under every *or*—the right *and*."

"Eye of the Storm, Pescadero Coast, 1972." In a winter of record rainstorms in Northern California, Cesar Chavez undertook a twenty-four-day fast in support of United Farm Workers' boycotts. The poem also honors an earlier farm workers union, the Federated Agricultural Laborers Association. In 1939, Filipino labor leaders Francisco Varona, Macario Bautista, and Lamberto Malinab led the first successful strike in Northern California's coastal fields of celery, garlic, and Brussels sprouts.

"The Resurfacing of Solano Avenue at the Millennium." *Night in Fog* is the English name of a film compiled of original Nazi footage of the concentration camps.

"*O Sun*, 2003" draws its energies from the largely ignored, but very large, public protests in US cities during the autumn and winter preceding the 2003 US invasion of Iraq. The poem recalls an unattributed news photograph I tacked to the wall of my childhood bedroom. Taken in Danang, Vietnam, a soldier holds his dead companion.

Some of the poems in the section "Haven, If It Is Haven, Gives" are in conversation with Emily Dickinson: "Quail" with "He went quiet as the dew / From a familiar flower"; "Vigil" with "Sleep is supposed to be, / By souls of sanity, / the shutting of an eye"; and, "Passing through the Aperture" with "It was a narrow time, / Too jostled were our souls to speak."

"We Shall All Be Changed" takes its title and most of its italicized phrases from the Recitative for Bass "Behold, I Tell You a Mystery" and the Air for Bass "The Trumpet Shall Sound," both from Part III of G. F. Handel's 1742 oratorio *The Messiah*. Two other italicized phrases are from J. M. Bischoff's 1901 *If God So Clothe the Grass* and Gustav Mahler's *Adagietto, Sehr Langsam* ("Very Slowly"). The fourth movement of his Symphony in C Sharp Minor is quietly driven by dissonance.

"A Stranger Is Met by Shapes of the World." Wislow and Motlawa are rivers passing into the Baltic through Gdansk, cradle of the 1980 Solidarity movement. Though in Poland the strikes were followed by a period of enforced martial law from 1981 to 1983, the early, nonviolent shipbuilders' protests played a significant role in the eventual collapse of Soviet control over Eastern Europe.

ACKNOWLEDGMENTS

I am glad to thank the dedicated editors of publications in which these poems first appeared, often in earlier versions:

Alehouse Review: "Lark"
Antioch Review: "*Your Mother   He Said*"
Beloit Poetry Journal: "Quail"
Comstock Review: "Elegy"
Denver Quarterly: "Asylum," "Being Read," "departure," and "her father's death in her body"
Cedars: "Embers of the Day," "Linseed," and "Passing through the Aperture"
The Missouri Review: "Interregnum," "A Traveler Is Met by Shapes of the World," "Confessions of a Tactile Kleptomaniac," and "A Way Back to Life"
The New Republic: "Eye of the Storm, Pescadero Coast, 1972"
Nimrod: "My Brothers," "Our Passing," and "*That Sunday Afternoon   She Said*"
Parthenon West Review: "Between Pages of the Dictionary"
Portland Review: "Cleaning Out the Garage in 1968"
Prairie Schooner: "Humpty in Our Hands"
Salmagundi: "Beyond All Tenderness"
Southern Indiana Review: "Unrepeatable Poem"
The Southern Review: "Atop Zugspitze"
Switchback: "The Music Inside"
Sycamore Review: "A Traveler Is Met by Touch"
Tampa Review: "The Disappearing Doors"
Tor House Foundation News: "The Resurfacing of Solano Avenue at the Millennium"
Witness: "Die Rote Jacke" and "From the Hold"
Women's Review of Books: "Vigil" and "Reservoir at Uvas Canyon"

"Interregnum," "Asylum," "Being Read," "Between Pages of the Dictionary," "The Music Inside," "Eye of the Storm, Pescadero Coast, 1972" "Lark," "A Traveler Is Met by Shapes of the World," "A Traveler Is Met by Touch," and "A Way Back to Life" appear in the chapbook *Radiantly We Inhabit the Air* (Seven Kitchens Press, 2011), which was chosen by Eloise Klein Healy for the Robin Becker Prize.

For tangible support in the making of some of these poems, I am grateful to *The Missouri Review*'s Jeffrey E. Smith Editors' Prize, Money for Women / Barbara Deming Memorial Fund, Squaw Valley Community of Writers, and Summer Literary Seminars, St. Petersburg, Russia.

Special thanks to Cynthia Hogue for selecting this book and for her foreword. I also thank Francesca Bell, Judith Butler, Forrest Hamer, Robert Hass, David St. John, Dean Young, and my family, especially Bessie Hutchins.

Tender the Maker is in memory of Bruce Allen Hutchins.

Christina Hutchins is the author of *The Stranger Dissolves* (2011),
a finalist for the Lambda Literary Award and Publishing Triangle's
Audre Lorde Prize, and two chapbooks, *Radiantly We Inhabit the
Air* (2011), which won the Robin Becker Prize, and *Collecting Light*
(1999). Her poetry and essays have appeared widely, including in *The
Antioch Review*, *The New Republic*, *Salmagundi*, *The Southern Review*,
The Women's Review of Books, and in volumes by Ashgate, Columbia
University Press, Milkweed Editions, HarperSF, and Houghton Mif-
flin. Awards include *The Missouri Review* Editors' Prize, the Annie
Finch Prize, two Barbara Deming awards, the James Phelan Award,
and fellowships to Villa Montalvo Center for the Arts in Saratoga and
Summer Literary Seminars in St. Petersburg, Russia, where some of
the poems in *Tender the Maker* originated.

Hutchins holds degrees from University of California, Davis, Har-
vard University, and an Interdisciplinary PhD from Graduate Theo-
logical Union, and she has worked as a biochemist, a Congregational
minister, and a professor of theology and literary arts. Her scholar-
ship focuses on poetry and philosophies of creativity, particularly the
work of Alfred North Whitehead, Judith Butler, and other critical
theorists. She served as the first poet laureate of Albany, California,
where she lives and teaches independent workshops.

THE MAY SWENSON POETRY AWARD

The May Swenson Poetry Award, an annual competition named for May Swenson, honors her as one of America's most provocative and vital writers. During her long career, Swenson was loved and praised by writers from virtually every school of American poetry. Winner of a MacArthur, a Guggenheim, and many other awards, she left a legacy of fifty years of writing when she died in 1989. She is buried in Logan, Utah, her hometown.